"Life And Passion."

KATHYRN MARTELL-MACKENZIE

authorHOUSE®

AuthorHouse™ LLC
1663 Liberty Drive
Bloomington, IN 47403
www.authorhouse.com
Phone: 1-800-839-8640

Published by AuthorHouse   07/17/2014

ISBN: 978-1-4969-2801-6 (sc)
ISBN: 978-1-4969-2802-3 (e)

Library of Congress Control Number: 2014912856

Contents

"Dedication"

By
Kathyrn Martell-MacKenzie

<u>"Life And Passion."</u>
This book is dedicated to my Mother Mrs. Frances Lillian MacKenzie; Nee: Morgan also to my Aunt Eleanor Cummings Nee: Morgan; Two beautiful strong women of great courage.

This book is also dedicated to my daughter Trina Kemp and her 3 lovely boys Kody Johnathn, David, and Kirk Andrew also little Jake. This book is also dedicated to my son Matthew George Christopher Scott Jacobs his beautiful strong wife Starla and my lovely granddaughter Georgia Adelle Jacobs. May God Bless and keep you all.

Love,
(Mother) and Grandmother
Kathyrn Martell-MacKenzie

Grandma's House

Coming "home" to Grandma's House...
makes me think of gingerbread houses
apple pie and something "good"
always cooking...
there is a old tattered sock...
hanging in the corner,
but you can bet the fireplace...
always seems a trifle bit warmer...
      at "Grandma's House."

The Christmas tree is sparkling
with joyous splendor...
Children's faces seem to glow
somewhat brighter...
      at "Grandma's House."

Someone is always knocking...
at Grandma's House...
This year... it will be the mailman,
possibly the milkman, and oh,
"Yes" the "<u>Spirit</u> <u>of</u> <u>Love</u>" knocks
"quite often"... at
      "Grandma's House."

"The White Dove of Peace."

I release the "White Dove of Peace"
for mankind in the year 2014.
Let your hatred and revenge flow
away like hot lava pours away
from the volcano...

If your fellow man asks you for
change... give not only from
your change purse but give from
your heart as well.
If you are judgemental of another
human being because of their skin color,
take a knife, cut your own arm,
cut his arm, you will find we
bleed "One Color" as a human
race.
Take the "time" to care for
our fellow man before "Time"
takes us!!!
The "White Dove" will fly free with
his message of peace only when
mankind puts his fellow man first
and himself second.

On the "Wings of Pegasus" the
White Dove must be released...
to fly free for eternal peace
for all mankind.

"In The Park at Midnight."

Come, we'll show you the little
mountain, they said...
It was grand tour time...
I seen the waterfall as a blind
man would see it...
I "listened" to the night sounds...
The stillness, the birds communicating
back and forth with their shrill
calls...
"I" would be a stranger now in
Hong Kong, he said...
"I know how you feel, I replied,"
I never had thought of it before...
Until I had moved and was a
stranger...
Now it was my turn...

I could familiarize myself with the
Vietnamese refugees...
The feeling of caution and sensitivity...
Of new surroundings, new
        atmospheres...

Yes, we as a human race must
be adaptable,
We must train ourselves, we never
know...
When we may have to use it.

"Non-Conformist in 2014."

I got my hair cut, all my "<u>straight</u>"
friends praised me...
I felt like it was some major
accomplishments... my hair used to
be to my waist...
It was also "<u>my</u> <u>companion</u>" when my
husband was not present... I used to
play with it and fix it up with
ribbons and bows... I could have
put bows and ribbons on "<u>him</u>" he
might have looked prettier...
but "pretty is a pretty does" and
he did some <u>pretty</u> "<u>non</u>-<u>pretty</u>"
things to me...
If you don't wear a business suit, cut your
hair short, have bible studies 24 hours
a day and marry a white man who
is a doctor or a lawyer you don't
fit into our "<u>Conformist</u>" Society
even in 2014!!! Well hey, ladies...
I'd like to dye my hair, red, green
and purple wear a dress with gold
& glitter & purple sequins on it.
Don't forget my leather boots!!!
And my motorcycle helmet please!!!
And oh <u>P.S.</u> if I want a roll
in the hay with a black man
because, Quote... "<u>He's really hung</u>"...
Then ladies you can clap for me
as this "<u>Non Conformist</u>" <u>gets laid</u>!!!

Alone at the top of the world.

"Writer."

"Writer!"...
Your heart is like a raging blizzard...
You cannot see the pages in front of you
Yet like a horse with blinders on...
You trudge on...
Your pen (your sleigh)
Your thoughts (your master)

And the "Crack of the Whip" urges you
on...
Writer... well your heart ever find a
resting place...
"Damn you master!!!"
The lashes sting my very soul...

"Writer!"....
Sleep and you are not friends...
You walk beneath the pale moon...
And your master smiles down at you...

"Writer!"
Put your sleigh in the barn...
for the storm is over...
My "Master" is quiet for now!!!

"Jack Fish for Wine."

I got a jackfish today...
they're clean, "Good" jackfish,
I wouldn't give you no shit...
Some pickerel toe, give me a
couple of bucks...
for a bottle of wine...

How many "Good" Jackfish
hit the frying pan for a
good bottle of wine?

This is the "<u>North</u>" and the
"Bottle of wine"...
has become......
The RED MAN'S BLOOD.

That's Amourè (That's Love)

When you feel like a child...
and are a little bit wild...
That's "<u>Amourè</u>"... That's Love...

When you are light headed...
as a "Dove"...
That's Amourè, that's love...
When you feel your spirits soar...
And your heart like a lion roars...
That's "Amourè", that's "Love."

When you pull your hair out
and you scream, yell, cuss and
shout...
That's Amourè, that's "Love"!!!

When you are old and gray...
And he still wants his way...
That's "<u>Amourè</u>", That's "<u>Love</u>."

When "<u>Death</u>" comes for you...
And he hollers...
          "Take me too"...

That My <u>Friend</u> is <u>Amourè</u>
That is "<u>Love</u>."

"Don't Be A Puppet On A String."

Ladies don't let that wedding ring...
Make you a "puppet" on a string...
Remember you can't have everything...
Don't forget to let your soul sing...
Don't be a "puppet on a string".....

You say you love me... let me go..
Let me have some freedom
For my soul...
Don't take the life out of me...
Cause I can't stand it if I'm not free...

Like a seagull you pull my wings apart...
Like a Gladiator you tore into my heart...

Your arrow pierced me right through..
And now "It's My Turn" for
leaving you.
Ladies don't let your wedding
ring... Make you a puppet on a
String...

Well, it's time this puppet ran away..
Because she got her soul back today!!

"Take The Time."

There was a old handicapped
woman set on fire in the park
the other day in broad day light...
At first the police officer thought
it was a pile of garbage...
"Until the pile of garbage
started to moan!!!"
Surely someone must have seen
this helpless old woman being
attacked in broad day light...
"Surely" "Someone" could have
"Taken The Time" to intervene.
        Chopped off hands and limbs
in Freetown, Africa all over Diamonds
United Nations has finally Taken The Time
to intervene. A woman runs naked
into the street, hands her baby to her
neighbour before her abusive husband
shoots her and the other children. The
neighbour said I used to see her with
black eyes & bruises, if only I would
have Taken The Time to intervene she
still might be alive.
        I am proud to say that I took The
Time to visit both my parents when
they were alive and my neighbour
took the time to phone the police
when I was being abused.
        And any time that I see a woman
being abused or poverty stricken
people, I will "Take The Time" to help.

Advice From A Seagull

Choose carefully in life with whom
we associate...
for God grants us wisdom, do
use it with care...
Choose your friends carefully...
Do not let this world make you
have a heart of steel...
for God grants us a heart to
feel with...
Perhaps rich men are kings on
earth, however we don't die to
our rank or our bank account...
Death has no favourites...
Take time to enjoy the beauty
of a flower or a morning
walk...
For life is like a handful of
sand, one minute we're here, the
next minute we're gone to join
the thousands... millions of other
grains of sand in this world,
so perhaps, we as a race, mankind in
general, perhaps mankind isn't as
important as we tend to think we
are. Sometimes we doubt that there
is a God because of the cruelty that
happens in life but remember the
beauty of a blue sky, the flight
of a seagull and like the sea gull
we must "soar high with life."

Letter To William Shakespeare

I am to receive the "<u>William</u>
<u>Shakespeare</u> <u>Award</u>" for my writing...
So I must get to know you, Mr.
Shakespeare and the <u>only</u> <u>way</u>
for me to get to know "you"
personally is by your "<u>Legacy</u>"
<u>Your</u> <u>Writing</u>.
          I see you were not a selfish man
Mr. Shakespeare for in your will you
also remembered "<u>colleagues</u>" and <u>neighbours</u>
besides your family. Nowadays we are
lucky that we're not killed by our
neighbours. You were a "Papist"
until the day you died... We differ
there William... I shall probably
worship "<u>Jehovah</u>" God and Jesus Christ
his son until the day I die. Like me
your life was not without controversy
and like me you held your own.
You were hot blooded, got your young
wife pregnant when she was a minor.
Like me, I too have been led astray
by my passionate nature.

May "<u>My</u> <u>Spirit</u>" as a Fellow writer
"<u>Always</u>" Be "<u>Entwined</u>" with your
spirit my fellow writer Mr.
William Shakespeare.

Wisdom

Alone at nights with no man
to call my own...
I think of past lovers...
Some of whom I could've married...
I remember one, who said I don't
want to fuck you, I want to make
love to you...
Yet he came like everyone else...
and I felt like I had been fucked,
"<u>not</u> <u>loved</u>"...
My girlfriend who is in thirties...
said we are getting too old for
this bar scene... We cannot compete
with the nineteen and twenty year
olds with their tight sweet asses
and firm breasts...
I feel oldness lies in the soul...
My soul is not old yet, it has
just become wiser...
And my "<u>Wisdom</u>" tells me to
"<u>Go</u> <u>home</u>."

"Who Are You?"

Who are you to be so bossy?
"Little Indian Chief!!!"
Can you command the wind???
Can you make the sky crash
with lightening and roar with
thunder?

Can you cause me to feel "rain"
upon my face???

You are "Just A Man" and "I" am
"Just a Woman."

It is time that you show some RESPECT
not only for your "Wife" but for
"Our Creator" who has much
more "Power" "Wisdom," "Courage"
and "STRENGTH" that either
"You" or "I" or "Mankind"
period could 'ever' hope to
possess.

I Need To Know

I need to know...
if I marry you...
Will you still rub my aching
feet and caress them with care...

I need to know...
Will you tie me to my bed post
while you run away with my
money?

I need to know...
Will you rant and rave with fury
if another man looks at me with
desire in his eyes...

I need to know...
Will you still have a heart of gold...
When my body is withered and bent
and the years have made me old...

I need to know...
Do you love me as much as I
love you ???

If the answer is... "<u>Yes</u>", then
that is <u>ALL</u> I need to know.

Yesterday

Yesterday, I walked across the snow,
where only the animals of the
wild dared to go...
Then I sat down on the river bank,
all quite alone...
and took a moment to stare out
into the distance only to see...
that there was a man on the opposite
side of the riverbank... staring out...
just like me...
He seemed to float through the air...
as... he lifted me over the hills...
until he set me down in a gentler
place still...
it was called "Bethlehem" and then
I was given the command, "Rise,"
my little one...
You must begin to worship and praise

It was if suddenly, the world was set free
and all mankind was glistening with
purity...

Such a beautiful experience it did
seem.....
Surely, it was not just a dream...

To Jesus On The Cross

My Spirit entwines with yours...
My Spirit suffers your pain...
That unbearable pain...that you
suffered on the cross...
Yet, I walk silent.....
Once, I placed a flower on the statue
of Mother Mary... holding a baby
lamb in her arms...
The flower was made out of stone
Like the statue...
I look at my poster of 4 male strippers
They remind me of statues with their artificial poses...

Where shall a man find a woman as
faithful as Mary Magdalene?
Where shall a woman find a man
with a love as great as you Jesus
had for the common people...

Perhaps the answer is nowhere, nowhere,
Nowhere On This Earth.

The Crocus

As a little girl, I rushed to the
hillsides... As soon as spring
came and the snow disappeared...
their beautiful velvet heads would
appear... and I would rush to scoop a handful to
bring home to my mother...

They would be proudly placed in a
bowl of water,
their velvet heads bobbing up and
down...
Somehow, I found such peace and
contentment in the picking of the
crocus.

Today, traffic abounds me,
Deadlines have to be met,
The clock on the wall seems to
be ticking faster all the time...

I dream of rushing to the Hillside...
To Pick...
"The Crocus"

Like A Stranger

Like a stranger... I wished you a
Happy Birthday... not really
caring whether you had a good
birthday or not...
You have not changed...

I cannot love you, now, or ever
It is all a game to be played...
in order to survive...

Yes, to live with someone you don't love
is as bad as being a paper machet
doll or a porcelain doll,
made of expensive China,

The phony smile never wears off,
      until......
The doll topples off of the shelf,
and falls to the floor...
Shattered in a million pieces...
Never to smile again...

Like a stranger, I smiled, a stranger,
a stranger... Your wife.

"To My Son, My Daughter."

Did I give birth to you???
"My Son" with gorgeous blue eyes
My beautiful blonde daughter...
With her rich Chinese boyfriend?
And modern sports car...

Well, I hope you both go really far...
But remember... no matter how rich
you are... Even if you become a
Famous Movie Star...
"<u>Fame</u>" is a fleeting thing...
Here today... gone tomorrow...

But "What" we <u>might do</u> for our fellow
man may bring <u>us</u> and <u>them</u> great
<u>Joy</u> or <u>Sorrow</u>.

With these "<u>Words of Wisdom</u>" I depart...
Judge not so much of your fellow man
With <u>Societies</u> standards but ...
"<u>Feel</u>" for your fellow man with
       "<u>All</u> <u>Of</u> <u>Your</u> <u>Heart</u>.??

"Infatuation."

People looking inside a glass window
At the shiny red firebird...
"Ah" mmm –– wouldn't you like to be
the owner of that baby...
the crowd murmurs to each other...

The owner of the firebird slid into
his new car...
He felt very important, very powerful
But, be careful, "<u>Power</u>" can be very
dangerous ... Remember Charles Manson.
A little blonde girl gasps in awe
at the beauty of the new dollie before
her covered in lace, she's in love
with it. All of her mother-hood
characteristics come forward...
To love it to mother it. A fantasy now
later on in life a reality ... Will she
love her new dollie then? A wedding
night, the champagne bottle is almost
empty. The bride was already drunk
with love. As she looked into her
mate's eyes she knew she had
captivated him...
He was "infatuated" by love...
But so had the Widow Spider
Captivated her mate... for awhile ... .
Ahh.... "<u>Infatuation</u>" can be
       a Dangerous thing........

"Old Poet In A Shack."

Old poet, old poet in a shack...
You better watch your back...
That your "mean old man don't
attack...
For he's "meaner" than a one eyed
snake...
And there's $$$ dollars at stake!!!

"Old poet", "Old poet" in a shack...
Who cares for you? And you think that
beggar standing on the street... you... think
he doesn't feel lonely too??? Don't be a fool!

I live with my animals you see...
Now maybe I get kind of lonesome
Because they don't talk you know...
But that's much better than suffering
My old man's blows.

"Old poet", "Old poet" in a shack
please don't turn your back on me.
For I have always loved you...
I will set you free for I
am your Lord you see.

To A Dear Old Friend

You phone me once every two years...
My dear old friend...
You say, "Hi!" this is Andy, your
dear old friend...
I say, "My dear old friend, if you
are such a dear old friend,???
Where were you when I was lonely?
When I needed a friend!!!

My dear old friend... Where were you?
When I cried out at nights?
And wondered how I could make it
through another day?
Where were you when I needed somebody
to give me comfort... And that word
"<u>Love</u>" that is almost extinct...
Like the dinosaur...
Love, yes "Love," Where were you
Andrew Suknaski? Hiding out in
your damn wood mountain hills,
writing "<u>your poems</u>" still searching
also for that extinct dinosaur...
Well, my dear old friend, I gave
up the search a long time ago...
      All that is left is the bones!!!

"A Letter To Heaven."

Today "fate" stepped once again
into my life...
Out of the mist... memories leaped
up to surround me...
Engulfing me, my father's
ghost dined with me tonight...
Some people called him a drifter
But "Most people" said he had a
good heart, I ran into a man
who was my father's friend.
I decided that "Fate" must be playing
a role in this scene but what the
role was I didn't know.
My daughter joined me, she did not
get to know her grandfather while he
was alive on this earth...
"Yep, "Ford" your father was a
okay guy" his old time
friend said to my daughter and me.
I could feel the clouds lift from
my heart when my daughter smiled...
and yes dad although you had
your moments like everyone else
in this world...
I'm sure when your grand daughter
smiled tonight, that it was "A-Okay"
(with you.)
        My love is with you dad.

Mother And God's Bouquet.

Picking crocuses in the spring...
Picking brown eyed Susans that
matched your eyes of brown...
Never having many material things
but your love and warmth spread
to others... like the morning sun...

"What?" kept her so alive and vibrant!
Ready to handle whatever life threw
her way...
"Where?" did that enthusiasm come
from?

From the heart, from the soul,
and from the flowers...
"God's flowers!!!"
Mother, when it is your time
to go.......
You shall be part of the best
bouquet there ever was... to pick
The bouquet in Heaven, "God's
Bouquet."

Our Pioneer Ancestors

We must remember our pioneer ancestors... How they fought, struggled, and died... so that their great grandchildren and great - great grandchildren must fight to keep our society a democratic one and when something is not right when there is poverty... We must change it to prosperity where there is hate, we must show kindness, and most of all, we must show "<u>Respect</u>" and "<u>Respect</u>" for our <u>environment</u>, and our <u>fellow</u> <u>man</u> if we follow these <u>guidelines</u>, I am sure that (our pioneer ancestors) shall (<u>not</u>) have perished in vain!)

To My Husband
    Thomas Joseph Martell.

"Eagles" "You And I."

Tonight... my dream will bring
Wisdom on eagles wings...
We will fly together into a silver
sky...
Freedom shall carry us so high...
We will kiss the air over Mother Earth
Where the wise women have been
since birth...
With the four winds, we shall
drift,
The gliding power, the "Eagle's
gift...
With grandmother moon we will
light and learn the secrets of
Grandfather night...
We will love and touch each other's
wings through the pines...
Just like them we shall stand through
the hardest of times...
We will dance on the mighty sea and
ask her how old she may be???
For the buffalo we will sing a
song to bring them home where they
belong. The willows shall wipe away
our tears and quiet our fears...
We will fly together with the
Spirits far above...
"Tonight" my dream will bring...
"Eternal Togetherness" and Love
on Eagle's Wings.

MEN And Their PENIS

MEN...
"M" stands for Meanness
"E" stands for "Everlasting Heartache"
"N" stands for No Heart, No
Caring, No Love, No Support.

PENIS

"P" The "P" from a man's
penis has brought me nothing
but "Pleasure"

"E" The "E" has been the "end"
when you have "climaxed."

"N" The "N" is for No Feeling
from your Heart (not the
Penis'es fault)!!!

"I" The "I" means "I" shall
love you and your "PENIS"
forever.

"S" The "S" is for "SEX"
"Pure" "Delightful", "Beautiful"
"SEX" with Your "PENIS"
And Beautiful "YOU."

Searching

Searching... like a lighthouse
keeper... I shine my light into
the dark on the cold still waters
of the night club.......
Searching... a shark comes toward
me.....
It circles a bunch of dolphins
and goes in for the kill... .
I am left to swim in the ocean
for awhile ... the ocean, the ocean
of life... Searching, searching the
ocean of life... For a husband
or a wife ... Ah well, the search
goes on ... Catch a wave.

Starvation

You become an animal, looking for
something to devour .... You want to
hang on to your morals .....
"Hunger" has no pride...
You are lucky you know... that you
live in Canada where you can take
a item of value down to the local
pawn shop or you have a food
bank to go to......
In many countries.... Death is a
welcome friend...
A Welcome end
To "Starvation."

Living

Off to work she goes... struggling
to make a living...
She comes home to her children,
her cat the bills and living...
At nights she wonders about the
man she married....
How he adored her when they were
first married....
How he adored the children...
Now he pays no child support...
She wonders about "living"
Her teenage daughter mouth's off
to her mother... She feels she knows
all there is to know, but she doesn't
know about "Living".... Let a
single mother try to earn a few extra
dollars to support her family and not
declare it to the "System" and you
wonder "why" the word "Justice" was
ever developed...
Ah, but that's living.......
Perhaps, my dear teenage daughter
will not think she knows everything
when I speak to her in twenty years
down the road ..... and like the
setting sun, wisdom has touched
her soul... and with time, like
all of us will have experienced...
"<u>Living</u>."

"Be Careful My Girl."

Searching for that lover of mine...
Hoping that he'll be the one...
Until the end of time...

Hoping that he'll really love me...
Just for me...
Not what I can give him financially...

It is a dog eat dog world out
there and the wolves out there
will devour your very soul...
If you let them... but you can't
let them..... no you can't let them.

So use caution my girl for
it is a tough old world...
And "Be Careful" when
you're searching for that lover
of yours...

Advice from a mother who loves
you.

"Robot - Motion."

Robot Motion on disco night...
Turn left... turn right... .
Beep... Beep... Sorry sir...
I don't have a name....
I'm Robot-Motion playing the
Disco game.....

I glimmer of eye shadow and
ruby red lips and boy baby...
I sure can shake my hips...

But my eyes show no emotion
at all...
I just count the money as my
back faces the wall...........

Robot Motion on disco night...
Robot Motion, turn left... Turn
right.... I'm sorry sir.......
I don't have a name.....
I'm Robot Motion playing the
Disco game...........
Beep, beep, beep, sorry sir.....
Beep, beep, beep, sorry sir......
I don't have a name......

"Memories Come Crashing In."

It's four o'clock in the morning....
And without any warning......
Your "Memory" came crashing
in...... What a sin... what a
sin...
What a sin when old memories
come crashing in...
What am I to do???
All I <u>can</u> <u>do</u> is just remember
you....... once in a while.
Once in a while, people will see me
smile......
When old memories come crashing in.

Now I'm a wife with a husband
and a life......
But every once in a while.....
Your memory comes around....

"<u>Too</u> <u>many</u>" Memories coming around!"
Hey, I think I will drown...
Throw me a life raft....
I'm down town...........
                              Swimming once again......

"Life"

We go round and round.....
One day up.......
One day down.....
That's "<u>Life</u>"

We can't have everything we
want........
Sometimes, "Old Memories".....
They haunt ....
That's "Life."

Take a husband, take a wife....
Let's hope you don't have too
much strife......
That's "Life."

Have a child or maybe two.....
After all your mother
Gave birth to you.....
That's life... that's life.....

In your grave at 62, 52, 42, 22
No in your grave at 2!!!

Sometimes that is "<u>Life</u>."

To "Art"

"In The Land Of The Midnight Sun."

In the land of the midnight
sun.........
I want to see our children run...

In the land of the midnight sun...
I want to watch the peaceful waters
flow.....
In the land of the midnight sun...
I want to watch our children grow...
As our love will grow.....
Beneath the ice and snow...

In the land of the midnight sun
Come grow old with me.....
In the land of the midnight sun....
We shall live eternally...
In the land of the midnight sun.

"God Created The Creatures."

First, God made the heavens.......
then the oceans... then the earth...

Then God created the "Creatures,"
He made the birds with silken
feathers so that they might glide
through the air with ease.....
He made the horse with strong
hooves so that they might carry
a heavy load.....
He made the elephants huge and
heavy... so that the "King of the
Jungle" might have respect for him.
(Mr. Elephant). In the "Animal
Kingdom" he created the Perfect World
and then......
God created man and woman......
And "Our God" carries a Heavy Load
on his shoulders and in his heart.
Do not despair my Lord for there are
those "humans" who appreciate your creation
of a flower..... . and every time
a newborn child is born.....
There is hope ..... That another
Mother Theresa or Martin Luther King is
breathing the "Gift of Life."
Ethiopia, dying children, I cannot stand the
pain, Canada, U.S.A. Hong Kong.... starving
people!!! What??? is the answer???
Is it simply to create another human race this time human beings with "Hearts
and Compassion." And "God created the creatures."

"Mannequin"

Like a "mannequin" I spin and
turn and my body burns....
in memory of what we had...
"Too bad" "too bad" "so sad" "so
sad" "so sad"....
Oh well, I shall begin again....
You know why?

Because I'm a "Mannequin" a
"Mannequin." One thing about us
"Mannequins" we may fall down
but we "Never" fall over....
We're luckier than a Four Leaf
Clover!!!

Our faces show no expressions
at all... We're just plastic
emotionless dolls... turning
around and around and around...
Our feet never touch the ground...
It is safe to say that a "Mannequin"
I shall stay.....
"Deep" inside of myself, my heart is
no longer displayed on a shelf....
I now have a heart of steel......
I no longer feel...... You can
"toss me," "throw me" on the ground!!!
I will never break!!!
Because I'm the toughest "Mannequin"
they will ever make!!! I'm the
toughest "Mannequin" around!!!

"North" Or "South"

Sitting in my comfortable townhouse,
with wall to wall carpet and color
t.v. I feel the urge to roam
again.... There is no challenge
in watching soap operas. I feel
the urge to see how real people
live again, tragic people, the
people of the north.....

The farmers of Saskatchewan are
taking the government to court
for 54 million in wheat payments...
The Northern Indian eats bannock,
hoping for a better life......

The north has beautiful pine trees,
The south is hot and dry, people eat
macaroni & cheese here and go to the
food bank..... is there really any
difference between the north and the
south?

In China there are wall to wall
people like my wall to wall carpeting
But in Canada there are wide open
spaces galore and resources...
Why must there be starving people
"North or South" Well perhaps the
Parliament buildings need decoration
again!!!

"Old Rubber Tits."

There is a story...
and it is true...
For I would not lie to you...
It is about a old dog...
She was as white as snow...
And everywhere that "Old Rubber
Tits" Went ... the tales were
sure to flow.........

Now you might ask how did this
dog acquire such a name?
Well, she slept with every type
of dog from St. Bernards to
Shepherds even a Mexican Chiwawa!!!
Yes, she was quite a dame!!!

She had spotted puppies brown puppies,
black puppies, white puppies, puppies
of all colors... Tales went around
and around... and when she walked
old rubber tits, well her tits hung
to the ground!!!

So this is why I call out in utter
dismay to you young girls
of today...
Do not become like "Old Rubber Tits
I pray!!!

The Windegoe Of The North

In Northern Canada again,
I jogged out to the bush planes
on the outskirts of town...
Rich dark soil, like chocolate
cake.....
Perhaps..... devils food cake....

For this is the part of the country,
where the Windegoe *she devil.....
Sometimes... roams...

Still at nights when
the wind howls in the north
country.....
You think of the tale of the
Windegoe and the trapper....

One "Kills to live" but
The "Windegoe" lives to kill...
"Tourists" are like "Caviar"
to the "Windegoe"

"Welcome Tourists" "Welcome" to
the North......
Ha! Ha! Ha! Ha!..........

"Goodbye Mom."

With laughing eyes and a
winning smile.....
I know it won't take but a
little while.....
For boys to notice her,
and want to carry her books
home from school........
She laughs, her carefree laugh....
Gives me a hug, and calls me
a dear old sentimental fool.

Now, it's Mom, How is my hair?
Tell me what should I wear?
Am I gaining weight?
Gosh, I hope Johnny's not
going to break our
date!!!

Than, it's "Goodbye Mom".....
as they shut the white picket gate.
"Goodbye Mom."

Ode To A Friend (Les)

He was a combination, a true friend
like him you don't find......
His mind held the potential of a gold
mine,
I can remember when we were closer
that year than brother and sister,
the two of us starving to death
in a mass of concrete buildings
and traffic...
Street kids, teenagers, punkers, sure
they're different, but one thing they
are is survivalists......
You were different, my friend, for
you possessed the spirit to give
without receiving.......
My friend, you gave me something
that I could never buy in any
department store.....
"That" was friendship, understanding
and love......
I doubt if anybody would ever have
believed us, if we told them......
We never did make love to each
other..... except with our "<u>hearts</u>."

"Love Song"

Have you ever heard a love song
that stirs your emotions so
strong.....
Let it take you to the edge,
the utter brink.....

Have you ever heard a love song...
It will make you sit and think...
and bring you to the edge, the utter
brink......

Then you might close your eyes....
and come to realize......
that single isolated tear....
that shocks you.....
with a terrible fear.....

Then the pain can often be too much
when there is "<u>no one</u>" around for
you.... in the middle of the night
to touch... to touch... to touch...

Air - Canada

Air Canada in the morning.....
Ladies & Gentlemen, welcome aboard,
you are about to throw up at 0800
hours, we are flashing a no
smoking sign, that is in case
the plane crashes,
We assume no responsibility
for your death,
It was that last cigarette that
did it,
You just "had" to have that last
cigarette, didn't you sir!
Yes sir, our main responsibility is
our passengers, In case of emergency,
kindly pull the lever at your left,
hold the oxygen mask over your face
not your mother-in-law's face,
"Sir!" Seems we have a sadistic
passenger on board here,
Please fasten your seat belts, our
seats are "Quite" expensive, in
case of a crash we don't want
to lose them,
Yes sir, our main responsibility
is our passengers.
This is Helena, your stewardess,
please relax, and "enjoy your flight."

"My Life."

"My life" involves two children
and ten thousand things to do,
"My life" involves sex......
when I get lonely...
like food when I get hungry...

Alone, wishing I was elsewhere,
comforted by someone's loving
arms...

"My Life" involves wishing, hoping
and dreaming... that someone
would care enough to share...
"My Life."

AIDS

Like a skeleton, he lay there,
chest caved in... Like a suken
souffle, eyes bulging from moon
craters that once were eye sockets...
"<u>Nurse</u>,"... more water please!!!

Scenes of a beautiful blonde flashed
through his memory, a beautiful
blonde with never ending legs, and a
set of cherry red lips, oh what those
lips didn't do to him.....
The bar was crowded, he couldn't
believe his luck when the most
beautiful blonde in the whole place
asked him to dance...... and dance
they did, later at his place,
they were still dancing......
in bed, it was pure passion.....
animal lust out of control.....
The nurse comes in, changes his I.V.
She is pretty and blonde.....
Suddenly her face changes......
She becomes a skeleton, a laughing
skeleton...... that says... Tough
luck buddy, you should have
picked a virgin.....

Aids, roared the skeleton, aids and I
are old friends.......
Ha! Ha! Ha! Ha!................

Prison Is A Place

Prison is a place where you
write letters and cannot think
of anything to say......

Prison is a place where you
gradually write fewer and
fewer letters and finally stop
writing at all.

Prison is a place where you can
go "for months" without feeling
the touch of the human hand,
or a kind word. It is a place
where your friendships are shallow
and you know it!!!

Prison is a place where you
loose respect for the law.
The Law, Raw and naked,
twisted, and Bent, Ignored
and blown out of proportion
to suit the very people who
enforce it.

Prison is a place where you wait
for a visit (A promised visit)
and wait..... and wait... and wait...

"Prison is a place like no place
in this world. Stay out of
"Prison" My fellow man!!!

"Inside The Looking Glass."

Inside the looming glass, I see
a woman......
whose dreams will probably never
come true....
I see a woman whose hair will
become faded and grey.....
Whose dreams might become a thing
of the past..... if she lets them...
If she lets them......

Still I continue to dream and think...
I think of Hollywood and wonder if
I will ever get to see the sights.....
I wonder if there will ever be a Clark
Gable in my life??? or if my
knight in shining armor will
come riding in on his white horse
to rescue me from this life of
boredom and sadness..........

But "<u>I</u> <u>dare</u>" to dream and out
of such dreams has come greatness.....
John F. Kennedy dared to dream....
Martin Luther King died in body,
not in spirit, but his dreams
"<u>NEVER</u> <u>DIED</u>"!!!
So I shall continue to dream and
"<u>This</u> <u>Woman</u>" will "<u>NEVER</u>" give
up on her dreams!!!!

"I'm Just A Country Gal."

I'm just a country gal,
Yeah, that's what I'm going
to stay........
I'm going back to the country....
Where love is true and people
haven't forgotten how to pray...

Well, I'm just a country gal,......
The city is too cold for me.....
I have to live in wide open spaces....
Where life is wild and free......

"Yeah!" I can ride my horse....
And make love in the sand,
Wake up in the morning time....
To hear the birds singing a
Country rhyme.....

Smell the clean fresh air......
Live off the land.... in my underwear
I don't care......
Because I'm just a country
gal,
The city is no place for me.....
So, if you miss this country gal,
You know where I'll be.

"Tough To Play The Game"

I could leave this marriage
with a lot of pain.......
But what good would that
do "me?" What would I gain?

I know I still have a lot of anger
As hard and as cold as stone,
I know there are times I miss
you and times I am so tired of
being alone......

I could be very bitter full of revenge
and hate... but why should I let
those emotions affect my fate?
For I know I am destined to be
great......
And to help my fellow man
while I am here on this earth
"That" is what I consider my
self worth.

I know I can be hostile but I
can also be fair. I can also be
understanding and I can care.

I am just a normal person, my
feelings are the same......
I am just like any other human
being..... Sometimes in life.... "It
just gets tough to play the game."

51

"Fuck Them," Feed Them Fish."

He was a big man with
a jolly laugh,
Nice to work with...
And when anything would go
wrong, he would say,
"<u>Fuck</u> <u>Them</u>", Feed them fish.

Now I think that no matter
what happens in my life,
be it death, destruction, even
if the damn nuclear button
were to be pushed tomorrow...

Then I would say, "Fuck them!"
Feed them fish.......
And my family and I would
be with the greatest gentle
man of all... Sweet Jesus!!!
Amen.

The "One" and The "Only."

When you're down and you're
lonely.......
And you don't know which
way to go......
Turn to the "<u>One</u>" and the
"<u>Only</u>" ......

The "<u>One</u>" for which your "<u>Heart</u>"
yearns......

When times are tough.......
And you've had enough.....
Don't you ever give up!!!

Just remember "<u>The One</u>.'
That died for you and for me....
And pick yourself back up!!!

"<u>Courage</u>" "<u>faith</u>," and "<u>wisdom</u>"....
are... <u>what</u> make me "<u>strong</u>"....
          and
"**Angel wings**" will carry me home
To be with My "<u>One</u>" and
"<u>Only</u>" "<u>Forever</u>" in <u>Eternity</u>!!!

"My Writing."

Will "my writing" stop the poverty
in this world? I think not.
Will "my writing" stop the rebels
chopping off the hands and legs of
children in Freetown, Africa
all over greed for Diamonds.???
I think not.
How about the homeless people
dying on the streets in Toronto?
Will "my writing" warm your
bones or warm the homeless
people (their bones) on cold
winter nights?
If "my writing" "encourages you" to
give to that street person a few
dollars, If "my writing" encourages
you to be kind to old people and
encourages in you a hatred for
child abusers, wife beaters, rapists and
murderers, "good" is all I have to say!

If "My Writing" encourages you
to "Love Your Fellow Man"
despite his skin colour or whether
(he) or (she) is rich or poor
young, old or crippled, if "My
Writing" teaches you to Love God
our Lord and "respect" "Our World"
of trees animals and "Beauty"
"Then" It is My Writing."

"Fame and Fortune."

Fame and fortune......
are their goals.......
They wait in line .....
Like hungry souls....

For "Fame" and "Fortune".....
He's been here now......
For two years..... Waiting.....
Waiting...... for "Fame" and
"Fortune"

It's going to come.........
He just knows........
He can feel it.......
In his toes.........

Fame and Fortune.......
Can feel it in his toes......
But I won't wait.....
For fame and fortune
Because "Fame" and "Fortune"
won't wait for me.

"Friendship"

School days.... Laughing ways...
Winning smiles.....
They'd walk a mile.....
Together in "Friendship"

"Graduation" a goodbye tear...
Move on to a new career....
Life held a little "Fear".....
But they still had "Friendship."

Married Life ... He took a wife...
She passed away today....
"She" phoned to say......
Be "Strong" "My Friend"
That's "Friendship"!!!

A single rose he placed
today.... and as he walked
away.....
He turned around on final
time to say to her......
"That's Friendship."

"Secretarial Life."

Here I sit on my lunch hour,
Feeling very much like a wilted
flower.
"Yes Sir", "No Sir", "Maybe so Sir"
"Hold a moment Sir,"
"Not me Sir!" "The telephone, Sir!"

That's the office life....
Eight until four....

Fifty–five words per minute,
Invoices galore.....
Boss is down your neck,
Until you close the office door,
"Goodbye Sir!"

At The Office

A tiny thing that someone said...
"Gee Honey", I'm glad it wasn't
the kids....
> Tenderness, a falsified tenderness?

The "<u>Wife</u>" is called "Honey"
The "<u>Secretary</u>" is a doll, a cutie,
> a play-thing...

I wonder.... if my husband acted
the same way.....

"<u>At the office</u>!!!"

"Just Me and The Old Eagle."

Just like me the old eagle
was in need of repair...
Somebody had shot him in the
face and injured his beak,

Just like me getting a new set
of dentures the eagle got a
"<u>new</u> <u>beak</u>" from a kind
hearted soul.

The newscaster joked that now
the eagle would have to use
polygrip to keep his beak together!
Well, I would be willing to give
that eagle a case of polygrip!!!

We could split the case of polygrip
between us and the old eagle
and I could live together happily
ever after.

"<u>Me</u>" with my new dentures and
"<u>The</u> <u>Old</u> <u>Eagle</u>" with his new beak!!

"Peace Poetry."

My dear fellow human beings, make
every effort to live in peace...
Politicians do not harden your hearts
against the poor and the oppressed...
Let our leaders heal our nations
Do not forget our most important
resource of all, "Our children."
   We must all be peace keepers of
our own countries. <u>No</u> <u>Country</u>
must be allowed to kill their own
people or murder their own children.
   We must respect human life no matter
what the age, race or color or status
of that person.
   The good lord is the creator of all
people, rich, poor, black and white.
   We owe it to God as a human race
to respect human life and live in
peace and harmony together in a
world that is so lovely.

The Key word is "<u>together</u>" "<u>together</u>"
"<u>Together</u>" We "<u>can</u>" stop the fighting.
"<u>Together</u>"... We "<u>can</u>" stop starvation.
   By Growing more crops and raising
Livestock.... and together we as a
human race can live in peace
and harmony, "<u>Together</u>."

"For Male Pigs."

I hit my wife gentlemen
I'm proud to say,
That I hit my wife,
When I was having a bad day,
When she didn't listen or do
exactly as I wanted her to do...
I would hit my wife gentlemen...

Well, I'd even hit my dog too
Yeah, I quite the man people
would say, quite the man...

If a woman is smart and has
a mind of her own
Well that's a reason to hit her too!

Yes, I'm quite the man gentleman!!!
I just haven't figured out
What kind of a man, gentlemen
What kind???

I think I have a soul gentlemen
But tell me where the hell is
my soul???
"Where gentlemen, where is my
soul???"

For "Male Pigs Only" or this poem was written
for men who abuse their wifes!!!

"White"

"Just A Squaw."
He tried to teach me... not
to swear in Cree.....
I swore anyway!!!

He told me that I was just a
"Squaw", and he was a "Chief"
so... this "Squaw kicked the
chief out!!!

He beat me, I survived!!!
He drank and left me home
alone by myself but guess
what???

This "Squaw" doesn't mind
being by herself, I like
myself.

This "White" Squaw will swear if she
feels like it!!!
            And this "White Squaw" might
just some day run for "Chief"
While the so called "Chief"
might just run period!!!

"Youth."

They say we dress funny...
We're weird and doesn't
that kid wear a earring in his
ear? He must be a druggie!!!

Look at those worn out sneakers!
And wasn't that Scott smoking
pot!!! Behind the bleachers!!!

Mark rolled his car today!!!
and Kelsey, she just went away...
to the city... Tsk .... Tsk
What a pity!!!

Karen, she had a son, well....
Tsk... . Tsk... . it could have
been anyone...
What's done is done.

"Don't talk" about the youth
that Graduated today...
Just talk about the negative....
Never ever talk about
The "Positive Aspect of Youth"
And we wonder "Why"???
"Youth" goes astray!"

"Oasis"

He came to me, young and
willing...
I could have said no....
Loneliness does funny things to your
soul....
And your morals....
Like a camel in the Arabian desert
I drank eagerly from your lips...

You were my "oasis".....
Once before, I wrote a poem for you,
about you....
When you were a boy-child...
Now I write again....
You are now a young man...

Let your heart nor your soul
be troubled....
For "<u>someday</u>" a young girl
shall come to you.....
       And "<u>she</u>" shall be your oasis

How Do You Know?

How do you know what I like?
When you're not home!!!
Night after night!!!

How do you know how I feel?
When you're not around to ask?
And you expect this love to last!
Ha!

Well, I've got news for you...
I've had enough of these
Lovesick blues...

So I'll be moving on....
And someday when I'm gone...
You'll be thinking of me...
But baby, you'll be just a
part of a very bad, bad history!

There is No Inspiration

You said that maybe I would be
inspired... by your visit, to
write another poem....
My inspiration fails me as
I listen to Madonna...
singing "Material World".....
once again I realize what a
"Plastic Society" we live in!!!

There is "no inspiration."
"In A One Night Stand!!!"

"I Want To Party."
I want to party, forget all my
troubles and woes....
The never ending bills, what the
future holds for me....
I want to dance naked in the
sunlight...
Feel the breeze in my hair, not
worry about what to wear....
Feel the sunlight on my shoulders,
Lay back and look up at God's sky...
Wonder about the universe.... and
why, why, why???
There is so much pain...
I see the children's faces, as I
lay back under the blue sky, and
I cry, "Lord, How I cry!" when I see the
children that starve every day...
I don't feel like dancing in the sunlight...
"I don't want to party!"

Dedicated: To Kirk Andrew Hansen. (My Grandson)

"Hey, Little Brother."

Fists up, fighting for his rights,
as tough as his older brother,
Following in his footsteps....
just enough......
Until he learns the path himself...
To make his own footsteps....

There is a softness
there is that boy,
A kindness of heart
that in later years,
Will make people remember him...
When it is time for friends to part.

A squaw wrassel in the dirt...
Just to prove he's tough enough
To hold his own.....
When you're a "boy"....
If you win......
It doesn't hurt!!!

Hey, Little Brother

Fists up, fighting for his rights
As tough as his older brother,
Following in his footsteps,
Just enough...
Until he learns to tread the path himself...
To make <u>His</u> "<u>Own</u>" footsteps.

There is a softness there in that boy...
A kindness of heart,
That in later years,
Will make people remember him...
When it is time for friends to depart...

A squaw wrassel in the dirt
Just to prove he's tough enough...
to hold his own...
When you're a "boy"
"If you win"
It doesn't hurt!!!

"Mirror."

"Mirror," "Mirror" on the wall...
Who shall love me when I am old
and gray???
When beauty fades away....

Like the maple tree when it's leaves
begin to fall ......
Oh well, this is the modern age,
people say, "Age" doesn't matter
at all!!!

So tell me why??? is that little
old Lady walking all alone???
And you say, you say that
Gray-Haired old man doesn't
have a home???

Ah well, this is the modern age,
people say "<u>age</u>" doesn't matter
at all....

I guess they are right in our
"Modern Society" "<u>age</u>" really
doesn't matter at all!!!!!

And the maple leaves continue
    To fall........

I Hear Canada's Voices.

I hear Canada's voices, the
different voices I hear...
I hear the voice of the waitress,
as she scurries about,
Hustling tips off of the table,
in order to support her children

I hear the voice of the mechanic,
greasy and tired at the end of the
day..... I hear the voice of the
mailman and the milkman
as they walk their daily routes,
I hear the voice of the secretary
trying to please her boss....
I hear the voice of the factory
worker, the truck driver, coming
home road weary... . I hear the
voice of the taxi driver, taking the
long route to make a few extra
dollars.... I hear the voice of the
nurse, understaffed and overtired...
I hear the voice of the salesclerk as
she rings up another sale, and smiles
a sigh of relief as she hears, "Five
minutes to closing, please take all
purchases to center aisle. I cannot
hear the voices of the poor, or the unemployed,
or the hungry voices of families standing
in line at the food bank.
Canada's voices!!! Ha! Ask the
Politicians !!! Ha!

"Look The Other Way."

Some patients get as many
as fifteen or twenty pills per
day......
Look the other way, look the other way,
some people were born in that
institution and shall die there.
Look the other way, look the other
way... Like drugged robots, they
move about trying to stay out
of the attendants way, in case they
are given that final needle
and don't make it through today...
Look the other way, look the other
way, don't you realize that you
are making a good salary?

Well, if a patient dies because of
a overdose..... Well hey, you
know what they say .....
Look the other way, look the other
way.... Abuse abounds in our
society, child abuse, senior citizens
are abused, patients in mental hospitals
are abused every day, but
                    HEY, I CANNOT LOOK THE
                        OTHER WAY!!!

"True Love."

There is love
There is Bullshit.......
"<u>SEX</u>" a roll in the hay...
Well, it's "<u>Sex</u>" but not "<u>Love</u>."

When I am old and gray,
And my bones are brittle,
Have sex with me then!!!

Then, perhaps, then it
could be called "<u>Love</u>."

"Meadow Lark"

I long to hear the beautiful
tune of the Meadow Lark in
the morning as the sun
rises to greet another day...
Beautiful spring mornings when
the pussy willows start to appear,
and the robins come near
with their bright red chests
so majestic like little soldiers
marching on the lawn....
Spring when the crocuses push their
heads through the snow and rose
buds start to open in full bloom...
Mr. Meadow Lark come sing to
me as I sit in this concrete apartment.
Set me free!!!

"Rock and Rollers."

Rock and rollers lead such
a empty life....
Even if they have a wife...
How many girlfriends do they
have on the side...
How many girlfriends do they
ride???
They ride their women
as much as they ride their
Harley Davidsons...
The only difference is you
don't catch the clap...
from your Harley,...
Like you do from that
chick called Marley...
In their older days they look
back to their glory days
and all the girls that they laid...
Ever wonder how much these
girls got paid? to hang behind
after the last show?
I think it was a lot you know.
Oh their glory days they
enjoyed them alright...
Oh those glory days what
a fright!!!
To be a old "Rock and Roller"
carries a Wild Legacy... I just
glad no "Rock and Roller" got into me!

The Dark Side

Why am I drawn to the
"dark side" The dark side
like a tunnel, that sucks
me down "further" and "further"
into a deep hole...
A "deep" "dark" hole.....
What lies at the bottom
is it my very soul or
is it?...... The Devils Home!
I sit here day after day and
my mind wanders away....
I throw a rope and bring it
back again....
Where have you been my friend?
Or are you my friend?
"No!" "No!" No!" I "scream!!!"
Because a "Friend" is "Somebody"
that is there until the end!!!
And you're not!!!
So I let the drugs do their
thing to kill the pain...
And I am sucked into the
"tunnel (Dark Side) (once again!!!)
Down... Down... Down...
Swirling waters drag me further
down below..... Where I'll stop,
who knows??? Into the
"Dark Side" for my last
final (ride) !!!
Welcome says Satan!!! Welcome to
Hell!!!

"Flowers."

Why do I like "<u>Flowers</u>"
So much???
Is it their sweet velvety "<u>touch</u>?"
That is "<u>sweeter</u>" than <u>any man's</u>
<u>touch</u> that I have ever known?
Oh their devine pure smell?
That doesn't smell like after
shave from hell???
Yes, "<u>Nature's</u> <u>own</u>" growing
in God's home.
God's home which is pure
kind and true... God's home
is the only place for me...
God's home where I can be
free... to be with my flowers.
You can have your traffic
and mansions and fast paced
living... all I want is
just God's land with a blue
sky the birds singing sweetly
and a field of flowers to lay
in. The petals of a flower have
never hurt me unlike "<u>your</u>
touch" The only flower that
ever hurt me was a "<u>cactus</u>"
and that was when "<u>I</u> <u>sat</u> <u>on it</u>
without looking first!" Not
the (<u>Catus'es</u> <u>fault</u>!") But man
<u>knows</u> what (<u>they're</u> <u>doing</u>) "when they
hurt you!" <u>I</u> <u>know</u>!!! <u>Testimony</u>
from a "<u>Flower</u> <u>Lover</u>!!!"

"Making The Days Count."

When I was younger...
I was wild and carefree
Now that I'm older...
I'm still (me) but I
am older and more wiser
And I take "Life more seriously"..
I know I only have so
      Much time left for to
put the dollar bill away....
      So it will be there for a
rainy day...
      Or when I am completely gray
with "Grayness" comes Wisdom...
and with (Wisdom), Peace,
Tranquility and Freedom
But a different type of
freedom than when I was
younger and carefree...
      A "Freedom" to know that
we have picked the right
choices in life and that
we are with our family
and can give them as much
love and kindness as we
possibly can and most of
all if we can leave
behind a Legacy of Love to
"Our Fellow Man."

"Into The Sunset."

Into the sunset we all must go,
off to meet our eternal maker ...
    Of whom some of us will
never know...
    But for those of us that do
know the Lord......
    We are the chosen few...
    The chosen few whose lifes
have been put through the
test of fire here on this
material earth... But
because of our belief,...
We have pulled through...
Pulled through where we
will suffer no more
No more abuse for my mom
or me because we will
both be off "Into the Sunset."
Where we both shall be set
Free...
We will be happy there...
    You see in that precious
place where the angels reside...
    While, here on earth men
will continue to live with
their material wealth and
puffed up pride
Puffed up pride & material wealth
that is not for me ... Give
me that final ride Into the
sunset where all souls shall be
Set Free.

"The Blanket."

Memories come to me... of
a "<u>blanket</u>" that was given to
us when we were newly
married... a gift from a
Native Chief, the Chief was
your Father and in your tradition
when a relative marries a
<u>blanket</u> is always given as a
gift. I remember your Father
well but did he also put
<u>your</u> <u>Mother</u> through a <u>Living</u>
<u>Hell</u>?
Was the <u>bottle</u> his <u>best</u> <u>friend</u>?
And did he go in place
when it was time for the final
end? I think as a Chief he
met our maker with dignity
and was welcomed like a
old friend.....
And will you be welcomed like
a old time friend.......
When it is time for your end?
God sees everything that we
have done.... when you beat
me and went with other women...
He seen "<u>everything</u>" you have
done... .
Oh, I have such "<u>pity</u>" for
you (<u>Native</u> <u>Chief's</u> "<u>Son</u>")

"Angels"

They say they are mythical creatures
who do God's work...
If you love the Lord and his son
Jesus Christ, you have nothing to
fear... For if you ask in prayer...
Jehovah's angels shall be near...

Near to you and near to you
to protect...
Do not fear because Jehovah's
angels do not neglect...

If you are lonely say a prayer...
You will sleep much more at
peace... in the Angels' care...

The Angels wings will cover you
at night...
Follow your heart...
And those angel wings will never
depart......

So now I call the "Angels" in
Jehovah's name to come down to
this earth to take away this
accursed pain.....
        Come down oh mighty Jehovah's
Angels"......
        Protect me, comfort me and give
me eternal gain....

"The Door Of Your Heart."

Tell me oh lover of mine...
How do I unlock the
door of your heart????
It is made of such solid
concrete I cannot seem to
move it...
And no key seems to fit...
I have tried everything from
love poetry to mirthless wit...
And still the door remains
locked...
Must I get down on my
knees and weep bitter tears?
Must I throw away caution
and all my fears???
For true love?

And how true is that "Love
on your part"???
Oh how true is that lover?
Dear Lover and friend of mine....
Is your love pure and divine...

For there is one thing you need
to know...
If I ever do "Unlock" The Door
of Your Heart....
        I Shall "Never" Depart.
        Ever

"What Can I Give?"

Where there is <u>no</u> <u>hope</u>
All I can <u>give</u> is <u>hope</u>
Maybe you know my words
Will never come true
Dear Brother
    But <u>you</u> <u>do</u> <u>know</u>
that I care for you.
I ask myself why a
Thousand times a day...
That the horrible things happen
in this world that do...
    And I only know that
Satan is alive & well & here
on this earth...
    And you must know that
too...
    But there will come a
time when we go to meet
our eternal maker and rest
assured he sees all we
have been through...
    And then the final decision
will be made as to what
to do...
    "With me and with you."
    For Jesus said let the man
that has committed <u>No</u> <u>Sin</u> be
the first to cast the stone...
    Of course not a pebble was cast...
    For the only sinless man was
standing there... Jesus gives us "<u>Eternal</u>
<u>Love</u>" what more can you ask???

"Shocking."

The world gets more and
more "<u>shocking</u>" every day...
      What can we do to bring
peace but pray...
      We pray and pray as
a human race... and
still Satan keeps us down
like little ants to be trampled
on...
Down in our place...
But hey they say the end
is coming near...
And then as a human race...
We shall know– "<u>Real</u> <u>Fear</u>."

For earthquakes shall come,
They "<u>already</u> <u>have</u>" and
split our homes in two...
      We shall loose our dearly
beloved... I shall probably loose
you (like the earthquakes) I
already have.
      Creatures of the deep shall be
awakened from their sleep like the
"<u>Oar</u> <u>Fish</u>' in Japan they shall
be tossed into the hands of mortal man.
      And when the final end does
come we must stand <u>firm</u>, <u>strong</u>
<u>tall</u> and <u>ready</u> to meet the final
<u>end</u>. With a shield of "<u>Faith</u>"
and "<u>Dignity</u>" We shall meet "<u>Our</u> <u>Creator</u>
my friend."

She Turned Down The "Tennis Date"

He liked the pretty ones... the ones
with real potential in life...
He was a choosy serial killer...
He didn't pick just anyone...

He chose college girls... career
women sometimes a young girl
just for a desert...

He was smart... most serial
killers are... look at Ted Bundy...
Serial killers bore easily they
are like sharks they are always
swimming in the waters
of women looking for that
next victim who is available.

Killing becomes just a matter of
routine to them like taking the
garbage out or running a
errand... Just relax they reassure
their victims it will be over
in a few minutes... They feel
nothing and the cries and screams
of their victims fall on deaf ears...

On the show "The Bachelor" the guest
won! A "Tennis Date" with "The Bachelor"
"She Turmid Down the Tennis Date.??
Instinct kicked in or may be it was God...
Something "Creepy "about" The Bachelor"
she felt. The "Bachelor" the "Shark" The "Serial Killer"!

"*Robin.*"

Robin, oh Robin, it soon
will be time for you
          To come a Bob... Bob... Bobbin
Bobbin along...
Singing your "Spring is here"
Tweet... Tweet . . Robin song...

          My mother always loved the
Robins you know and when
she seen them in her back
yard...
          She knew spring was near...
          And that's when a smile would
break out on her face and hope
would spring anew!!!

Spring would soon be here with
the Robins... bouncing among
the morning dew ...

So now when I sit alone lonely
at some park bench and I
think of all my mother went
through...
          Mr. Bob ... Bob ... Bob ... Robbin...
omes Bobbin along ... Singing
his Robin song... and I know
my mother is speaking to me through
that bright Robin breast...
          Saying be strong ... Be strong...
          And do for "<u>You</u>" "<u>What</u> <u>is</u> <u>Best</u>."

"Zinderella"

"Zinderella!" Why do you weep
so?... In your "Tower of Gloom"
You loved him so...
This we all know...

But do you need a man
who doesn't respect you...
And treats you like a old
shoe?

You "Know" the answer to that...
That is for sure...
So why is it that you feel
More pain you must endure...

And endure it you have for
the past ten or fifteen years...
Endure it you did...
While you shed countless tears...

All over a man who doesn't
know the meaning of love...
You kept trying... trying
until your white wings were
shattered like that of the pure
white snowy dove...

So all I have to say is ...
White Dove... White Dove...
Fly Away ... and Zinderella
Stop your weeping today!!!

"Disconnected"

Like telephone wires that
have been disconnected...
We as a human race
Wander aimlessly about...
Depressed... we take pills
to cure the depression ...
instead of turning to each
other... We are all
Disconnected... Depressed
Robots who rely on computers
for our companionships...
My computer is in my bedroom...
But it doesn't make love
to me at nights... and I long
for my husband for his touch
when we used to make love...
So for now Masturbation fills
the bill or is a substitute
a substitute for the human
touch as I have been
"Disconnected" from the
human touch for so long...
That I have almost became
a automated 2010 machine you
know a 2010 technological human
being who is "Connected" to
all the latest technologies but
"Disconnected" from the human
touch. Oh Husband of mine I hope
we reconnect so I can connect
once again as a Human Being...
Feeling ... Loving ... Touching ... I
don't wish to be "Disconnected"...

"It's A Blink."

Wah! It's a baby boy...
Eights pounds eleven
ounzes... with eyes of blue...
Wah!!! It's a baby girl...
Seven pounds... seven ounzes ...
With blonde hair that is so fair...
All the fairest in the land the
Lord declares...
So the single mother worked her
butt off to put them through
school.....
Now she sits in a old
folks home waiting for the
maple leafs to fall...
And the blue eyed baby boy
now 28 years of age hardly
ever calls...
The same as the baby girl
with hair that is so fair...
Why you hardly know that
she is even there...
The mother and grandmother has
already picked her coffin out...
White stainless steel with hand
painted roses on it....
Is lovely don't you think...
Don't you think???
The baby boy that doesn't call
or the baby girl that doesn't bother
at all... Ahh ... life goes by
so fast... Don't you think...

"It's A Blink!"

88

"The Richest Man In The World."

The richest man in the world
Is not someone who has a
billion dollars in the bank...
The Richest Man in the world
is not someone who owns
yachts and mansions and the
latest sports car...

The Richest Man in the world
is someone who sleeps peacefully
at night... Knowing they worked
honestly for their living and
never mislead anyone or
took advantage of the poor...

The Richest Man in the world
is someone who walks out
in the morning light dressed
casually not with a suit
and tie but walks among
the poor and the needy
and takes the time to attend
to orphan's cries...

Keep all your mansions and
your towers of gold...
For it is the man who walked
in sandals amongst the poor...
For it was "Jesus" who was
the Richest Man in the world...
I am told......

"Snow"

There is something about snow...
That brings a peace and tranquility...
as it blankets the hills and
valley... like a shepherd's cloak
protecting mother earth...

The freshness makes us want
to suck in more air...
Like fish swimming in a
Goldfish bowl...
We have been indoors
for too long... in our little
Goldfish bowls ... living our
little gold fish lifes...
Swimming around and around
in the whirlpool of life...

"Snow" brings back "Memories"
of Childhood days...
Tobogganing... skating on
the creek ... Carefree ways...
When we had not yet experienced
the hurts and heartaches of
adult life... when you become
a mother and a wife...

"Snow" makes me feel young and
fresh and alive... more alive
than when I was a married woman
"Snow" "Snow" "Snow" too bad
you have to go....

"Baseball"

Baseball seems to bring out the
youth in everyone...
      As we watch that young
grandson pull a slider into
home base ... we jump in
our grandstand shouting hurrah!
Hurrah! and reliving the days
when we were twelve or so
and took that final slide to
bring home a homer...

The smell of hot dogs fills the
air and fresh popped pop corn...
Although we know we shouldn't
be going off of that "special diet..."
We have to take that chance
and enjoy a hot dog and
a coke oh don't forget the
popcorn too...

Before we take that "<u>final</u>
<u>slide</u>" into the "<u>Final</u> <u>Home</u>
<u>Plate</u>" up in God's baseball
diamond ... Where the angels
keep the final score.

"Control"

"Control" can be used to
intimidate people...
But only if you let it...
You can use "control" to
intimidate others... but only
if they let it...
If we are disabled physically
and face challenges...
Our condition can "control"
us but only if we let it...
The government can "control"
us financially to a certain
extent but only if we allow
it and do not use our
"potential" to better ourselves.
We can become depressed because
of failed relationships money
problems and problems in
life in general but only
if we allow those feelings
to "Control" us and we
don't "control" the feelings...
"Control" can be used "negatively"
or in a "positive" way to
improve people's lifes...
        "Control" a very interesting
word don't you think???

"The Only One."

The only one that can
separate us from our love
for God and his son Jesus
Christ is "Ourselves!"

"People"

Some people are like donkeys
They have to be pushed and prodded
to get the job done...
You are like a balloon or a
kite you always were the
happiest when it was your
turn to fly away...
I got tired of hanging
on the string... to try to
make you stay...
You were like a stick of
dynamite... I never knew
when you would blow up...
Which caused my blood pressure
to rise...
I am now much more at peace
looking at beautiful blue skies...
I am lonely it is true...
But I don't miss that fiery
little dynamite stick... and
that kite that always flew away
or that stubborn donkey that I
never could convince to stay...
I guess I get more pleasure
in God's peaceful love and the
white turtle done...

"Courage."

"Courage" is speaking out to
wrong a injustice...
Even if it means risking your
life...
"Martin Luther King" had "courage"
to speak out against prejudice.
It may have cost him his
life ... But he did not die in
vain...
And today we have a Negro
African president of the United
States... what a shame
it would have been if Martin
Luther King did not have
"Courage" we would not have
had a African President today
who is such a strong and
courageous leader of the
United States...
"Courage' of John F. Kennedy
who also was not afraid to
speak the "Truth"
          "Courage" of Rosa Parks who
would "not" sit at the back of the
bus just because she was a Negro
woman.
          "Courage" of women who marched
so we as women would have the
"right to "vote" the same as men do..
"Courage" is a powerful, inspiring
thing. More people should have
"Courage."

"Mr. Nobody."

He walks downtown for
his daily stroll...
      He doesn't care about
money or things...
He's waiting for the Salvation
Army bell to ring...

Mr Nobody don't bend your
head so low...
For I've been watching you
wherever you go...
For if there's one thing
I can forget...
I was that girl that
you left...

Mr. Nobody, I'm sorry I
married somebody...

He walks downtown for his
daily stroll...
He doesn't care about money
or things...
He's waiting for the Salvation
Army Bell to ring...
Mr. Nobody....

I'm sorry I married "<u>somebody</u>."

"Come Meet The Big Spender."

Come meet the big spender...
He's one hell of a pretender...
That he's a happy man...
He'll take you out to
dinner and spend all he can...

He'll take you out for
Lobster dinner for $39.95...
And in between drinks you'll
bless the day you were
born alive!!!

But it is a funny
thing when the "Big Spender"
is sitting at home all
alone... and his money
is all gone...
It's funny but none of
the big spender's "friends" are
at home.......

Come meet the Big Spender...
He's one hell of a pretender
That he's a happy man...

"I'll Fly Away"

In between the pain and the
abuse..... She never stopped
believing ... that God would
send a angel to rescue
her... but it never happened
for Satan's Demons were
too busy laughing as her
Satanic daughter tormented
a old woman ... . Ha! Ha!
Ha! laughed Satan's Demons
torment her some more....
As they closed the fiery door...
And so a beautiful soul lost
the earthly fight...
          And was taken up above...
          But where she was going...
was where only God's
angel's abide and well
Satan's daughter "<u>Marybelle</u>"
I'd hate to be you on
your <u>final</u> <u>ride</u>...

Today one earthly angel
breathed her final breath
here on this earth...
But now she is with her true
friends her heavenly angels
where she laughs and smiles
"every day... singing, "I'll
fly away sweet lord, "I'll fly
away...

"At The Setting Of The Sun"

Tell me when I am old and
grey and my bones are brittle...
Will you still take my hand
and walk through this world
with me???

At the setting of the sun...
Will you still be the one???
To hold me close and
whisper those three little
words that every woman
loves to hear...
"I love you dear"....

At the setting of the sun...
Will you sit with me...
As we laugh at the memories
Some good some bad....
Some happy some sad....
But the main thing is we
can still laugh and
you will still be sitting
by me....
At the setting of the sun...

And when we are laid in our
final resting place and our
children stand around and say
the Lord's Grace... You will
still be by my side "<u>At The Setting
Of The Sun</u>" in our final resting
place.

"You Are One Wild Bird."

With air so bushy it
reminds you of a large
thistle on top of one's
head...

You are tall and lean
From your years of running
barefoot in Africa
You look uhh... very
very healthy....

And quite contented with
a happy smile upon
your face... and why
not??? You probably
have ten wifes that
you keep satisfied...

With a dong that goes
up to your belly button
built like a horse "Wild Bird"
you are probably quite satisfied
your dong attired in bright
canary yellow looks like a
pelicans peak between your legs...

But I can bet you are one busy
pelican you wild bird you and
you are the reason why African women
are such outstanding runners.
Because of "One Wild Bird."

"Roy Rogers," and Johnny Cash.

Roy Rogers was a good
old cowboy as he and
Dale rode off into the
sunset on trigger...

Do you think they are up
in cowboy heaven
Making everlasting movies?
You go figure....
About Roy Rogers, Dale
and good old trigger!!!

Just like Johnny Cash he
was a straight shooter
you don't find men like
them nowadays
Everybody runs their separate
ways...
When they married a woman
it was for life...

Nowadays men don't know
the meaning of the word
                    "Wife"
Wife to them is somebody to
cook and clean and if they
wish... treat mean...
The men now a days could
take a lesson on how to treat
your wife from Roy Rogers
and Johnny Cash.

"To Travel or Not."

My dear old Aunt has stood
by me... when others have not...
My dear old Aunt knows of the
hell I have been through...
        With "<u>you</u>" and "<u>you</u>" and "<u>you</u>."

So I am thinking of what
she said ... to come when the
weather is warmer to come
when her grand-daughter's
baby is due at a later date...

At all I think is does
time wait??? Does time
wait for anyone?

And so a decision has
been reached ... I answered
the question myself...
It is time I jump down
off of the shelf...
and wipe the dust away...

Pack my bag and go play.
I hope you have the <u>tea pot</u>
<u>ready</u>!!!

                                    Auntie Here
                                       I come!!!

"My Grand Son."

Probably his first smack in
the nose and my grandson
Kody Johnathn learned he
wasn't so tough...

It's a tough old world
out there Kody Johnathn and
if you're going to party with
the big boys that's what is
going to happen Kody Johnathn...

You have yet to learn that
a "quiet soul" is a "Wise
soul" and wisdom comes with
age I have done foolish things
also Kody Johnathn when I
was younger and didn't give
a shit now I "know" I am
lucky to be alive
Jehovah's angel was watching
over me but Satan's Demons
are also loose on this earth...
Be aware of that... "Fact"
And live your life with
"Caution" and "Wisdom"...
Words of advice to
        "My Grandson." Kody Johnathn
From a "Grandmother" who
(loves you) very very much!

"She Goes On."

Her brother beat her... Life
goes on... she goes on...
Her sister killed her mother...
whom she loved dearly...
"<u>Life</u>" goes on... She goes on...

Her husband ran around on
her raped her which ever
way he pleased to rape
her oh he never supported
her and he beat her also...

But hey life goes on...
"<u>She</u>" <u>goes</u> <u>on</u>...

Poverty is her daily visitor...
But she goes on...
So is loneliness no love no
sex no companionship crowded
living conditions and poor
health but life goes on...
and "<u>She Goes On</u>."

The pen is her best friend
when she <u>dies</u> her "<u>writings</u>"
will <u>live</u> <u>on</u>... and she will
be with her saviour and the
heavenly angels... "<u>She Goes On</u>"
into the "<u>eternal writers playground</u>"
"<u>She Goes On</u>."

About The Author

Kathryn Martell- MacKenzie resides in Canada on the prairies at present. She is not only a writer but a artist as well. Kathryn enjoys her family and the "<u>Simple Things</u>" in life. You can keep your City Lights...

The country is the only place for me bury me amongst the hills and the beautiful flowers...

God's Creations.

I hope this writing stirs your emotions then I will know I have written well.

Kathryn Martell - MacKenzie.

Author @
Copyrighted Internationally 2014.